THE ECONOMICS OF JOHN KENNETH GALBRAITH
A Study in Fantasy

If this book is representative of the intellectual vigor of the right, they are indeed fortunate to have moral majority and big money on their sides. Their case would never stand on its own merits.

D

The Economics of
John Kenneth Galbraith

A Study in Fantasy

SIR FRANK McFADZEAN

Centre for Policy Studies
London 1977

Centre for Policy Studies
London 1977

Soc
HB
119
G33
M32

First published 1977
by Centre for Policy Studies
Wilfred Street
London SW1
Revised Edition October 1977
Typeset and Printed by
Leighton & Lonsdales Ltd,
70 Glenthorne Road, London W6
© Centre for Policy Studies
ISBN 0 905880 00 5

Disclaimer

This paper is intended to be an authoritative contribution to the debate on current economic, social and political issues. The Centre for Policy Studies does not seek to express a corporate view through its publications, the authors of which are chosen for their independence and intellectual vigour.

—Who funds this group? Corporations

A doubtful commodity

iv

Contents

Read Galbraith
and you will see
what a shallow,
shrill attack this
book is on the
idea of Galbraith.
This book is a
prime example of
intellectual dishonesty:
Heavy on adjectives,
light on logic.

v

Contents

Foreword

by **Sir Keith Joseph MP**

It has been known for some time that Professor Galbraith was to be given the chance by the BBC to present a long and costly television series. His views are idiosyncratic and partisan. He does not support them with any evidence. No other economist, as far as I know, has supported them. Yet he is the guide whom the BBC has invited to conduct viewers on a ramble through economic and general history, arbitrary and partisan in its treatment of the past and the prescriptions it draws for the future.

The choice tells us more about the BBC than it does about economics. Since Professor Galbraith has become the current mentor of how to condemn the market economy without actually studying it, we sought an authoritative critic able to subject the Professor's assertions to reasoned analysis. We were fortunate in persuading Sir Frank McFadzean to undertake this task. He is uniquely qualified by a lifetime's experience as academic, civil servant, leader of industry and administrator to consider the Professor's theories. The reader will judge for himself.

Ken Joseph .

I. Introduction

It was once said of Hegel that he set out his philosophy with such obscurity that people finished by thinking it profound. A similar accusation could well be levelled at John Kenneth Galbraith. Not that his language is turgid. Indeed, from his Reith lectures[1] to *Economics and the Public Purpose*[2] his views have been set out in a racy and witty fashion, demonstrating a rare command of words. But one searches in vain for evidence to justify his lofty claim that he is actuated by a spirit of scientific enquiry and is above the time-serving motive he attributes to his fellow economists. Scientific enquiry implies a careful weighing of evidence, the formulation of testable hypotheses and respect for the rules of logic—but these are not the brightest stars in the Galbraithian firmament. It is his huge, almost Rabelaisian, entertainment value rather than any profundity of thought that has put him among the most widely read authors of our day. Yet it would be wrong to under-estimate him as a formative source of ideas. His beguiling prose style can easily so anaesthetize the critical faculties of the unwary that they finish by believing that he is making a new and vital contribution to economics.

Galbraith sees himself as the scourge of neo-classical economists and author of the blueprint which will solve all the problems of modern societies on an international scale. He labels his fellow economists "instrumentalists" because they are concerned with policy issues, whereas "the ultimate test of a set of economic ideas is whether it illuminates the anxieties of the time"—anxieties about expenditure on armaments, about income distribution on a national and international plane, about business—particularly big business—about the quality of consumer goods, obsolescence, about the environment, about economic growth and inflation. Although this widens the normally accepted scope of economics, the criticism which can be directed at Galbraith is not that he writes about these topics but the manner in which he does so. He does not elucidate, much less resolve or relieve, the anxieties. He exacerbates them. Part of his technique is to make sweeping generalizations, then admit some qualifications, which he then submerges completely as he deploys the generalizations in their full polemical splendour. Although *Economics and the Public Purpose* is an improvement on *The New Industrial State*[3] in this respect, any improvement is purely marginal. We still read that the control of prices in the planning system—as he christens the world of large corporations—presents little difficulty, only to learn that prices have to be set at a level "consistent with the need to persuade the consumer".[4] The first statement, on which Galbraith concentrates, is intended to convey the impression that planners in big business can determine prices as they wish. The second statement sharply restricts the price fixing freedom by underlining the need to meet the test of the market, but this is pushed into the background.

Galbraith's intellectual hauteur is of such noble proportions that he disdains to test some of his more exuberant generalizations against readily available information. Of course, he is too intelligent not to see that his sweeping approach has defects. With supreme, if unconscious, irony he assures us that "for the person who is resisting truth nothing is so convenient as the overstatement which becomes the handle for assault on the whole proposition." Quite so, but objecting to perversity of presentation is hardly resisting truth. Galbraith's form of presentation can in no way be regarded as a source of illumination for any topic.

Notes

1. *The Listener,* 17 November-22 November, 1966.
2. Andre Deutsch, 1974.
3. Hamish Hamilton, 1967.
4. *op.cit.,* p. 116.

II. The Importance of Change

Galbraith prefaces his analysis of the modern industrial state by emphasizing the importance of change. This may not be immediately visible to a younger generation brought up in an environment where moon flights, television, motor cars, transistor radios, tape recorders, and southern fried chicken are taken for granted. But to the older members of the community the changes—many of which have been brought about in their own lifetimes—have had a profound effect on the nature and quality of their existence.

A catalogue of change could cover almost the whole range of human activities. Unfortunately, complains Galbraith, the increased sophistication both of the end product and its method of production has not been matched by a parallel advance in the economic and social analysis of how the new industrial state operates. The difference between the market economy as traditionally taught and the underlying realities of business as it is operated in practice is not one of degree "but a difference which invades every aspect of economic organization including motivations to effort itself."

Although Galbraith illustrates his basic thesis by outlining the rise of the Ford Motor Company, the points he makes about its early history could apply almost equally to the formative years of large enterprises in other industries.[1] The relative simplicity of some of the earlier technological marvels had several consequences.

The costs of entering the business were not excessively high so that many individual firms were set up in the earlier stages of the development of—say—the motor car and the aeroplane. The simplicity of the end product meant that the degree of specialization was minimal. Aeroplane engines were adapted motor car engines and most of the constituent parts were of a common user nature. Thus no great harm was caused if a particular item was temporarily unavailable. Again, the time that elapsed between an idea, design and production of the end product was relatively short: *The*

3

Spirit of St. Louis for example, in which Lindbergh crossed the Atlantic, took only sixty days to build.

The advance of technology, says Galbraith, has changed a fairly simple economic structure. As products have become more sophisticated the lead-in time between the decision to build and the appearance of the end result has lengthened considerably. Factors affecting the lead-in time are: whether or not a new production line can be introduced in an existing building or whether it requires additional factory space; the amount of time, capital and effort that management can apply to a particular project and the industrial relations atmosphere prevailing in a plant—particularly the willingness of personnel to adapt to new designs and new systems. In some countries new agreements with unions, particularly where many are involved, can consume time measured in years rather than months.

The greater complexity of the end product and the means of producing it has resulted in a massive increase in the capital committed to individual projects; even where a corporation has manufacturing capability, the capital required for 'face-lifts' let alone new models, is still large compared with the nut and bolt operation inherent in the early vehicles. Not only has the direct investment in plant, property and equipment increased enormously, but so too has the amount of capital tied up in ancillary support equipment, stocks and work in progress, whilst striking the optimum balance between the interruption costs of shortages and the high cost of carrying large stocks has become a management task of growing importance.

The degree of specialization inherent in modern technology makes a very large part of the equipment incapable of alternative use and enhances the importance of co-ordinating a wide range of sub-divided specialist activities so that the end product, be it a motor car, aeroplane, gasoline or natural gas, is produced in the quantities and at the time and place required. A substantial part of the investment cannot be switched to another car or aeroplane, let alone other forms of engineering where the possibility of making a profit seems attractive. Mis-assessments are, therefore, costly.

Finally, in the early days, the consequences of failure, while of some importance to the entrepreneur concerned, were not really devastating in terms of finance or lost employment. Had the motor car for one reason or another been a failure, people like the Dodge brothers, who produced some of the original engines, would have had no great difficulty in switching their considerable talents and facilities to some

4

alternative product for which a profitable market was available. In Britain, too, had the internal combustion engine failed, the world of many original motor car manufacturers would not have collapsed around them. Nowadays, the risks involved in some advanced technology are so great that no single firm or group of firms could undertake them. It is what Galbraith calls the "compulsions of technology" rather than political ideology that makes assistance from the State inevitable.

There is nothing very new about all this: it has been well-known for a long time to anyone who has run a large corporation. Moreover, Professor Jewkes might well argue that Galbraith overstates the importance of change and that no solid evidence is produced to prove "that technical advance is now going on more rapidly than before or that the inventions of the present century are any more significant for mankind than those of the nineteenth."[2] But differences in this respect would be primarily matters of emphasis. When, however, Galbraith proceeds to describe how, in the light of these changes, modern economies operate, his views become controversial indeed.

Notes

1. Harry Miller, *The Way of Enterprise,* Andre Deutsch, 1963.
2. *Sources of Invention,* p. 195, Macmillan, 1958 (Second edition, 1969).

III. The Planners

The Technostructure

Galbraith argues that the complexities stemming from change have resulted in the industries set up by the founding fathers—the Fords, Carnegies, Rockefellers, Deterdings and so forth—passing inexorably beyond their control. The entrepreneurial corporation has been transformed into the mature corporation. As a consequence, power has passed into the hands of what he calls the technostructure—a conglomeration of managers, accountants, engineers, chemists, physicists, computer programmers, etc.—who combine to form the decision-making and planning process of a large corporation.[1]

Galbraith is very struck by the fact that in the mature corporation there is a sharp cleavage between ownership and control. Ownership lies with the shareholders who count for nothing in the day-to-day running of a large firm. According to Galbraith, the board of directors does not count for much either. "Power" he says "passes from the owners or their nominal representatives on the board of directors to the management of the corporation. And within the corporation, for the same reason, it passes down to the individuals who are actively participant in contributing their knowledge to the decisions." In other words, power does not flow from the top downwards. Power and decision making require information which flows in, is sifted, assessed and consolidated at lower levels in the technostructure. Men who hold high office in a large corporation are dependent on the technostructure for their information flow and technical knowledge. As a consequence, says Galbraith, they possess considerable powers of ratification but only modest powers of decision making.

The central thesis of Galbraith's argument is that "there is a sharp conceptual difference between the enterprise that is fully under the command of an individual and owes its success to this circumstance and the firm which, without entirely excluding the influence of individuals,

6

could not exist without organization." In *The New Industrial State* the division of the economy is between "entrepreneurial corporations"—where management and capital invested are substantially in the same hands—and "mature corporations"—where management is in the hands of professional operators with little or no financial stake in the business.[2] In *Economics and the Public Purpose* the division is between the "market sector" and the "planning system."[3] The market sector is the mass of small firms which Galbraith concedes are out to maximize their profits and, because they are operating more or less under conditions of perfect competition, are thereby maximizing the welfare of the economy insofar as it lies within their power to do so. But this "intellectually undemanding institution" of the market economy is inapplicable to the world of mature corporations where the planners, aiming to eliminate uncertainty, can insulate a company's fortunes from the fickle forces of the market and give it powers which make some of them "conceivably omnipotent".

The planners can achieve their objectives in several ways. They can integrate their operations vertically from the raw material to the final consumer product. Short of vertical integration the mature corporation can use its purchasing muscle to suppress the market. For many supplying companies the size and importance of the potential outlet to a large mature corporation are such as to render them co-operative. But not only do the corporate planners lean backwards to control the prices of their raw material supplies, they also lean forward to manipulate the consumer to accept what they care to produce at a price they dictate. In a rare concession to reality Galbraith admits that manipulation of the consumer is not possible in countries with a low standard of living. Once, however, they have a minimum of food, clothing and shelter, they fall for the blandishments of advertising which dethrones consumer sovereignty and makes them easy victims of a corporation with goods to sell. But advertising is only part of the great process of persuasion: the latter also embraces the development of symbiotic relations with other firms and governments so that it becomes in their interest to go along with the aims of the technostructure. Underpinning the whole edifice is the assiduous promotion of the growth ethic whereby society at large is persuaded to agree that economic growth is all that really matters and that whatever and whoever promote growth merit support —not least in public policy terms.

On motivation in the planning system, Galbraith argues that since the divorce between ownership and management in large corporations is virtually complete, there is no *prima facie* reason why the techno-structure should toil to maximize profits for a collection of faceless shareholders.[4] The motivations that drive the mature corporation differ from those of the entrepreneurs in the market sector. He maintains that the prime aim of the technostructure is survival. This entails preserving their autonomy through various planning activities and by abdicating their entrepreneurial status. They seek not to maximize profit, which can be dangerous, but to achieve only that *quantum* of profit which will meet shareholders' minimum dividend expectations and enable suffic-ient money to be ploughed back into the business to provide independ-ence from outside finance. Profit above this minimum level does not enhance the security of the technostructure but *per contra* profit below this minimum and, *a fortiori,* a loss would lead to intervention. As loss avoidance will take precedence over increasing profit, ventures where the prizes could be great but entailing the risk of failure will be avoided.

Galbraith rounds off his description by bringing into the picture the trans-national system. Since publication of *The New Industrial State* the so-called multi-national has become an essential part of intellectual equipment for would-be system builders. However, this provides no problem since the multi-national "is simply the accommodation of the technostructure to the peculiar uncertainties of international trade. It transcends the market internationally as it does nationally. It accom-plishes over a world of multiple national sovereignties what it first accomplishes within any one". The aims and weapons are basically the same.

From his analysis of the alleged power wielded by the technostructure in the planning system, a reader might reasonably expect Galbraith to argue in favour of stronger anti-monopoly legislation or to support some of the rather naive divestiture schemes currently going the political rounds in Washington. Far from it. He argues that the powers exercised by the technostructure should be elevated to the national level. Galbraith has no time for fiscal and monetary management: the mature corporation is immune to market restraints and will not therefore respond to such controls. In an age of inflation workers demand higher wages. Since the technostructure does not wish to provoke interference from the labour unions these demands are met and the resultant cost increases are passed to the consumer in the shape of higher prices. Once started the process becomes self-perpetuating and he sees the only solution as a thorough-going planning system with wage and price controls throughout the whole economy. He believes firmly that world economic activity is fixed and it is fixed by the factor with greatest inelasticity of supply at the margin. In Galbraith's world this happens to be the "planning system" But he does not want to unfix it: merely to transfer the process of fixing to economists like himself. Having chastised his colleagues for their neo-classicism he opens up for them an almost lyrical future signposted in language which would do credit to the advertising experts he derides. Let them enlarge their ideas about the content of economics and they "can embrace, in all its diverse manifestations, the power they now disguise . . . the problems of the world will be part of their system"—for they will be the ultimate planners. Tomorrow thou shalt be with me in paradise; the rest of us will be at the edge of the abyss peering into the Stygian gloom of George Orwell's cesspool full of barbed wire.

The Economist Kings

The perceptive reader will note from the foregoing that despite the strong whiff of Highgate Cemetery surrounding Galbraith, the dictatorship of the proletariat is ousted by that of the economist kings. It is probably true of any country that a concentration of economic power of the type he envisages would inevitably fall into the hands of politicians. This is particularly true of the United Kingdom where the long-suffering British have for decades had to endure the spectacle of the pseudo-intellectuals of the left wallowing in their near-gibberish about "forging a new Britain in the white-hot heat of the scientific revolution" and "storming the commanding heights of the economy" unable, apparently, to sleep because they are so restless with positive remedies.[5] Yet the evidence of history indicates strongly that once political and economic power are in the same hands the outcome is usually the tyranny of one or other of the extreme 'isms'.

Galbraith's sketch of the businessman in charge of a mature corporation portrays a citizen of rather wide-ranging specifications. In the market place he is a veritable tiger using his almost omnipotent powers to bend consumers and suppliers to do his bidding. When it comes to investment, however, he appears to have been born in the year of the mouse: he thinks only of survival and scurries timorously away at the mention of high-risk venture or the mere sight of one of the proud elite of the financial community who might interfere with his autonomy. If the businessman wields the enormous power that Galbraith gives him in the market place, it is by definition impossible for him to have an investment that produces no return. *Per contra* if the investment options open to him show varying risks and returns this indicates that he cannot have plenary powers in the market place.

The fact is that Galbraith's analysis of the new industrial state bears little relationship to reality. Every social market economy embraces a wide diversity of production units varying from small wheat farmers functioning in the classical tradition to near-monopolies—which are often public utilities. The bulk of the economy falls between these extremes with varying degrees—usually exaggerated—of market power. It is Galbraith's attempt to polarize the economy at the two extremes that leads, as we shall see, to so many overstatements and contradictions in his presentation.[6]

The Great Divide

Let us examine the sharp conceptual difference which Galbraith claims differentiates the market sector from the planning system. In his terms it is only in a one-man concern that an individual can be regarded as being fully in charge. When a business grows it is necessary to recruit someone to look after the sales, another the accounts and another the production. If expansion continues staff numbers will grow, functional delineations will increase and become more precise. In spite of his talk of "sharp" differences Galbraith is totally unclear at what stage of development a business leaves the entrepreneurial or market sector and moves over to the mature corporation in the planning system. In American terms he sometimes talks of the planning system as being composed of the three hundred largest companies but he has gone as high as the top thousand.[7] Mathematics are not his strongest card. Yet since the power, the disciplines and the management styles are, in Galbraith's analysis, so different between the two, the crossing of the Great Divide should be among the most important events in an enterprise's history. Yet, if you do not know where the Great Divide is, or how to recognize it, adjustments to the radically altered status could pose problems.[8] This is all very inconsiderate of Galbraith—unless of course the Great Divide only exists in his fertile imagination, in which case location problems for the rest of us are entirely understandable.

As soon as a business ceases to be a one-man band it has, in Galbraithian terms, created a technostructure. Employees will know things the owner does not, but the owner has knowledge that the staff does not possess; he views the problems from a broader standpoint and generally supervises, guides and co-ordinates their activities. Put another way, the private soldier looking out of his foxhole is likely to have more detailed knowledge of the terrain lying immediately ahead of him than either

10

his company or battalion commander. But, while this information could be vital to him if an attack develops, it is only important to the overall objective if it discloses some obstacle which might jeopardize the success of the mission. This information only gives the private soldier power in the sense that he has a choice of whether or not to pass it on to his superiors. The same is largely true of a well-run business. The technostructure regard the knowledge they possess as being the source of their contribution to a project; only in exceptional circumstances would they regard it, as Galbraith does, in terms of power.

In other places Galbraith uses the word "power" as if it were a function of size instead of being related to the alternatives available and to whatever additional external pressures exist.[9] If one of the multiple food chains were to raise its general prices above those of its competitors it would soon have to change its policy or close down. Its customers would switch their business to other stores, the hosts of Myrmidon would descend from price control, stern leaders would appear in local press and the shaggy manes in the House of Commons would be tossed around with careless abandon as the iniquities of the capitalist system were denounced in the resonant tones so often used as a substitute for factual content. In contrast the small store in an isolated village could probably raise its prices by a similar amount, and still retain the bulk of its 'convenience' customers. Nothing would be heard of price controllers or leader writers and, even if known in the House of Commons, it would evoke only a gentle shaking of the head and minimum re-arrangement of hair styles. Size by itself is no criterion of power in the market place.

"Control" is another word that Galbraith uses in a specialized manner. When contrasting the market and the planning systems he propounds the idea that unless a person is continually making decisions right down to the minutiae of an operation he is not in control of it.[10] On this interpretation only the driver of a London Transport bus or the helmsman of an ocean liner is in control. Of course, there is a sense in which this is true but most of us do not interpret control in this restricted fashion. Control in the normally accepted sense of the word consists in the ability to set the objectives of an organization; to intervene if the objectives are not being achieved or are not being achieved fast enough; or to intervene if there has been such a fundamental change in surrounding circumstances that the objectives themselves have to be recast.

Of course control can sometimes be lost. A physical failure in a communications system can result in a higher echelon of command losing touch with the development of events to such an extent as to undermine its ability to influence them. Failure to communicate the reasons for differing assessments of the nature and significance of basic information, or varying views on how to solve a particular problem, can only too easily result in a dialogue of the deaf within an organization. Or there can be such disillusionment or collapse of confidence in the leadership that positive or passive sabotage results in directions being no longer implemented. The organization usually loses purpose and coherence as a result.

Some of these problems arose very sharply in the Ford Motor Company towards the end of its founder's rule. They have also manifested themselves in the mature corporations. But they are not specific to business—they are inherent in organizations as such. They apply in substantial, if not equal, measure to the Roman Catholic Church, the armed forces, the civil service, the Boy Scouts and the Daughters of the American Revolution. Most of the bile and the rancour that Galbraith directs at business could equally be directed at the other organizations in our plural society. Although probably not using such grandiose phraseology they all require technostructures, they all require lines of communication and systems of control to make them function and achieve their objectives. The gibes that Galbraith makes about boards of directors—about the retiring company president's last flight on the private jet before passing into oblivion—could be equally applied in Britain to the Air Chief Marshal's last fly-past, the university Vice-Chancellor's last meeting with his Senate or a retiring Archbishop of Canterbury's farewell to his clergy.

It is easy to strike patronizing attitudes towards these events or the individuals involved. Indeed, sneering at established institutions has for long been the hallmark of the 'intellectuals' of the left—people, as Schumpeter put it, usually devoid of any practical knowledge of the issues on which they pontificate but who disguise this shortcoming by their command over the written and spoken word. They live on criticism, on criticism that stings; nor are they frugal in the distribution of their venom. Of course some of those who retire from high office will represent the epitome of the 'Peter Principle'—promoted well beyond their level of competence—while the sighs of relief at their departure could well emanate from a wider group than only those who move up the hierarchy as a consequence. But there is no necessity to be so tormented by envy and indignation to send them all, like the ghost in *Hamlet*, to their accounts with nothing but their imperfections on their heads.

12

Many textbooks have been published on the general problem of control in an organization: the span that one person can handle, the problems of communication, information flows required, the training necessary to fit people for higher management, the need to avoid 'soggy layering', the delegation of responsibility, and so forth. Much has also been written about management styles in large organizations—authoritarian, consultative and participative.[11] Some textbooks are directed at specific organizations such as governments, the armed forces or business. But one of the by-products of advancing technology has been a growing similarity in the problems with which some of the larger organizations in society have to deal. The equipment of an air force or an army poses many of the same problems encountered in a large industrial corporation For example, the organization chart of General Evans's United States Air Force System's Command, and the management tools he proposes to use as he re-inventories the Air Force's ageing stock of weaponry, are very close to those that would be used in a large corporation confronted with a task of similar magnitude. Given the fact that the basic issues are wider than business, how correct is Galbraith in stating that power flows in the reverse way from that implied by the ordinary organization chart and that those at the top have considerable powers of ratification but little in the way of decision making?

No doubt it is possible to find top management in all organizations who are indolent and quite content to wait for ideas and proposals to emerge from the technostructure. But it is grotesque to generalize. The objectives of most organizations are set by the men at the top while their attainment is almost invariably determined by a two-way flow of information and ideas through various levels of the technostructure. During the Second World War, organization could be given most of the credit for setting the scenes for various battles but their development was in many cases heavily influenced by the intuitions, judgments and personalities of a handful of men at the top. General Rommel must have been a sore trial to his technostructure (staff) in the Western Desert; his habit of moving up to the front line with his soldiers must have produced a certain degree of confusion in command channels. But the effect Rommel's presence had on his troops' morale will almost certainly have more than compensated for any disruption of the chain of command. There is no reason for assuming that, without Rommel's own contribution, 'organization' would have ensured the campaign's success. Probably, if only because of the weight of material, the final outcome would have been the same: the method of achieving it, the time involved and the casualties would have been different. Indeed, had there been any truth in Galbraith's approach it would have been quite unnecessary to replace so many generals during the War. If the function of the man at the apex of the organizational pyramid is only to ratify it does not really matter too much who wields the rubber stamp—indeed an ADC or a secretary might do it more effectively than a general or chief executive.

Galbraith relies heavily on the motor car industry to support his arguments, so let us look a little more closely at the trial of strength in the early 1920s between General Motors and Ford for market supremacy. At the material time the capital employed by the two groups was approximately the same; they were only in competition at the margin since General Motors concentrated at the upper, more expensive, end of the market while Ford practically monopolized the market in cheaper, mass produced cars. General Motors had been largely put together by William C. Durrant. As a result of his habit of buying shares on margins Durrant was squeezed in the slump of 1920 and had to sell most of his holdings of General Motors stock. Thereafter the Du Ponts, of chemical fame, became the main shareholders. Pierre Du Pont became chairman and chief executive officer, but the effective force in the organization was Alfred P. Sloan, soon to take over the principal role and hold it for twenty-three years.

In the case of the Ford Motor Company the end of the First World War found Henry Ford Senior with 58 per cent of the capital. He had a disagreement with the minority stockholders. Henry wanted to plough the profits back into the business; the minority stockholders wanted dividends. A somewhat complex struggle was finally resolved by Henry buying out the minority interests, thus becoming owner of all the capital.

General Motors' aim was to use the Chevrolet car to challenge Ford's supremacy in the mass market. This company succeeded in spite of the set back occasioned by the copper cooled engine but would probably not have done so had Alfred P. Sloan adopted the rubber stamping role suggested by Galbraith. At each successive stage he brought his influence to bear on the strategy that eventually put General Motors ahead of Ford in the number of cars produced.[12]

In Galbraithian terms Henry was probably doomed to lose the fight before the battle lines were even drawn. It depended on which side of Galbraith's "sharp conceptual difference" the Ford Motor Company was held to be. Although there was undoubtedly a technostructure,

Henry owned all the shares and, for good or ill, dominated the organization. If, because of this, Ford is regarded as an entrepreneurial corporation, falling therefore into the market sector, it will be subject to all the disciplines of the market place. This seems a bit harsh on Henry since he would have been competing with the mature corporation of General Motors with its "plenary" (another favourite Galbraithian word) powers to compel the consumer to take what it cared to produce at any price it dictated. Henry would have lost his chances even before the gong for the opening round had sounded.

Of course this only highlights the nonsense in Galbraith's artificial split of the economy. Both contestants were subject to the same restraints. General Motors won the engagement mainly because Henry insisted on meeting the competition of the closed versus the open car by tinkering with the model 'T' instead of designing a new vehicle. It was the entrepreneurial, not the mature, corporation that carried on for too long, trying to induce consumers to take a car they no longer wanted. It has never been suggested that when he tended the store anyone other than Henry called the shots; the same was true of Alfred P. Sloan, although he was more subtle in his approach, and his management style was less autocratic.

Managements of large corporations are a popular Aunt Sally for politicians and writers. A favourite description is 'self-perpetuating oligarchies'—a charmingly perjorative phrase, although it is doubtful whether many of those who use it understand its meaning. Here again the issues are much wider than in business alone: The Roman Catholic church, the army (in both its military and salvation versions), the civil service, and many other organizations could equally be said to be self-perpetuating oligarchies. The problem really distils itself into the best means of selecting and training people for high office. Galbraith is inclined to pooh-pooh this as of no great importance and giving little in the way of power to its practitioners. This is in contrast to one of the great pro-consuls of Empire, Lord Milverton, who, when once asked what was the most important function of a Governor, replied "the appointing and disappointing of civil servants".

From the time of the Webbs to Anthony Wedgwood Benn, the left in Britain has always underestimated the problems of management, probably because few of them have had any experience of it. Drawing organizational charts showing Chairman, Finance Director, Production Director, Sales Director, and so forth, while necessary, only states the problem. Organizations as such do not do anything; it is people who do things. The larger the organization, the wider are likely to be the variety of talents employed. The aim, admittedly not always achieved in practice, is to assign staff to the task which suits their talents best; to keep testing 'high flyers' in jobs of increasing responsibility with a view to finding their true level of competence. There is, of course, a very large area of judgment and luck does play a considerable part in an individual's progress, but nobody has devised a better system. Indeed, one of the alternatives—political patronage or nomination by government—has reached such a scale in Britain as to be a source of concern in spite of strong efforts by the Civil Service Department to bring some sort of order to the system. "In the hands of today's ministers are appointments to no fewer than 304 public bodies employing two million people at a cost to the taxpayer of £2,500m a year. Among them seven cabinet ministers have 4,223 jobs at their disposal worth . . . £4.2m a year . . . The Energy Secretary appoints some 200 people collecting £850,000 a year".[13] Recently it has become painfully obvious that the government has had great difficulty in filling various posts; there is still a sporting chance that opportunity may yet knock for Little Lord Fauntleroy and Caligula's horse.

Whatever the method of staff appointment, any organization will be successful only if its members are effective, if they see clearly the objective and, in spite of the many distractions and deflections, push through to its achievement. If the senior executives of an organization are not themselves effective but are content with the subsidiary role allocated to them by Galbraith, it is only a matter of time until the organization itself deteriorates as an effective entity.

Of course the difficulties in the way of removing chief executives—or prime ministers or failed academics for that matter—should not be underestimated. There are many examples—Henry Ford and Sewell Avery are only among the outstanding ones—where chief executives have clung to office to the detriment of the corporation they were supposed to be serving.[14] Although not justifying the mockery it excites in Galbraith, there are, of course, many instances where outside directors have failed to hold executives in check and shareholders, in turn, have failed to call the board to account. It is true, as Galbraith says, that business has become so complex that few shareholders have the necessary knowledge to challenge the management and that annual general meetings tend to degenerate into ritual dances. Such checks as there are tend to take place on occasions other than the annual general meeting. Quarterly, as well as annual, accounts evoke questions from the financial press;

meetings with investment analysts and credit rating institutions result in probing questions about the operations, financial health and objectives of a corporation; a greater openess in discussing problems and their solutions with members of the technostructure helps to contribute to a system of checks and balances. Nobody who has examined the system carefully would claim that it was perfect, but neither is our method of selecting, electing and removing politicians.

By using the phrase "entrepreneurial corporation" to describe the business entities in the market sector, Galbraith conveys the notion that these are the thrustful, enterprising elements of the modern economy. Examples can, of course, be found to illustrate this thesis. Yet it is only necessary for the reader to take an intelligent interest in the town or city in which he lives to see that the generality of such an approach is untenable. For every Sir Isaac Wolfson who builds up a Great Universal Stores group, hundreds of his contemporaries are content to jog along managing the store they either bought or inherited several decades ago. There are family engineering, foundry, transport and whisky distilling concerns that are ultra-conservative and change little over the years in either the product they market or in their management methods. Nor is it correct to suggest that entrepreneurial corporations have brighter, speedier and more alert managements than mature corporations. Some there undoubtedly are; but these attributes relate more to individuals and management styles than to size or the ownership of the capital. Henry Ford would almost certainly have behaved the same way whatever side of Galbraith's Great Divide his company had fallen or even if, during his tenure of office, it had passed over the invisible barrier. Likewise, Sewell Avery's hoarding of cash at Montgomery Ward's in anticipation of another 1929 crash, and Roy Hurley's obsession with short-term profits at Curtiss Wright had nothing at all to do with how the corporations were classified in Galbraithian terms. They had made their assessments of the course of action likely to be most beneficial for their corporations; and not for the first time they were both proved to be wrong.

Notes

1. (An extremely critical review of this argument appeared in *The Public Interest*, No. 9, 1967, by Professor Robert M. Solow, 'The New Industrial State, or Son of Affluence',—Ed.)
2. *op.cit.*, p. 92.
3. *op.cit.*, pp. 44-5.
4. (Professor Harold Demsetz, 'Where is the New Industrial State?', *Economic Inquiry*, March 1974, could find no evidence to support Galbraith's argument.—Ed.)
5. T.W. Hutchison, *Economics and Economic Policy in Britain, 1946-66*, Allen & Unwin, 1968; John Cockcroft, *Why England Sleeps*, Arlington Books, 1971.
6. Milton Friedman, *From Galbraith to Economic Freedom*, Institute of Economic Affairs, 1977.
7. Solow, *Op.cit.*
8. Professor James Meade, 'Is "The New Industrial State" Inevitable?' *Economic Journal*, 1968.
9. (For a critique of this argument read George Stigler, 'The Economist Plays with Blocs', *American Economic Review, Papers and Proceedings*, May 1954, pp. 7-14.—Ed.)
10. Friedman, p. 17, *op.cit.*
11. Douglas McGregor, *The Human Side of Enterprise*, McGraw-Hill, 1960; Rensis Likert, *New Patterns of Management*, McGraw-Hill, 1961; A. Maslow, *Eupsychian Management*, Irwin-Dorsey, 1965.
12. *My Years with General Motors*, Sidgwick and Jackson, 1965; John MacDonald, *The Game of Business*, Doubleday, 1975.
13. Robin Oakley, 'All Aboard the Gravy Train', *Sunday Express*, 1 August, 1976.
14. Richard Austin Smith, *Corporation in Crisis*, Doubleday, 1963.

IV. The Entrepreneurial Corporation

One of the many anxieties of our time that Galbraith fails to illumiate is precisely where entrepreneurship stops and gambling begins. Indeed, there is no objective set of rules that enables one to decide in advance where the dividing line lies. Not only do some corporations take risks which to others look the height of folly but even within a corporation there can be, and have been, sharply divided views on the commercial assessment of particular investments. It is only after, sometimes long after, the original decisions that it is possible to assess the financial consequences. In keeping the water-cooled Chevrolet engine in production, contrary to instructions, Alfred P. Sloan was proved by events to have been a shrewder judge than Pierre du Pont who, as chairman and chief executive of General Motors, was prepared to chance the future of Chevrolet, and his competitive position vis-a-vis Ford, on an air-cooled copper fin engine. It had fewer parts; as it had no water jacket it was cheaper to make than the conventional engine and in theory could out-perform it; but it was unproven. In the event the engine failed. It is, however, interesting to speculate what the relative assessments would have been had the copper-cooled engine been a success. Would Sloan then have been used by Galbraith as the archetypal product of a mature corporation interested in survival only, while Du Pont was made of more thrusting entrepreneurial material? The only trouble with such an analysis would be that both were officers of a mature corporation assessing the risks of a particular policy in a different manner.

Galbraith argues that the aim of the technostructure is survival; yet most decisions in every day life are not taken for survival reasons. The bulk of healthy people when they wake up in the morning know at the back of their minds that, provided they do not cut their throat when shaving, quaff hemlock instead of morning coffee, go up the motorway at 70 mph in the wrong direction, or pick a quarrel with the office Orang Utang, they are likely to see the day out. But let them be involved

19

in a 'glass inferno' or a multiple car crash and survival will come to the forefront of their minds and play a large part in their subsequent actions.

The same is broadly true of business where everyday decisions do not have a high survival content in their make-up. It is only in a time of crisis, or where the failure of a major investment decision could cripple the whole enterprise, that survival plays a role. But these are the minority of decisions and there is no evidence to support Galbraith's contention that they are more particular to the mature than the entrepreneurial corporation. There is certainly no *prima facie* reason why this should be so. If an individual's capital, as well as his income, is tied up in the same enterprise he has a twofold interest in its survival—whereas in normal times able members of a technostructure can obtain positions elsewhere with little loss or inconvenience. Moreover, some of the major errors of judgment which have raised survival problems—the Convair 880 and 990, the Edsel, the Rolls Royce RB-211, Burmah Oil's tanker commitment, and British Leyland Motors—were made by mature corporations and not, as required by Galbraithian analysis, entrepreneurial ones. The techno-structure in these instances had obviously forgotten that they should not take big risks. Conversely, in the declining days of his one-man rule, Henry Ford's near wrecking of the enterprise he created had nothing at all to do with pushing on to new frontiers with technologically advanced products that the mature corporations were too timid to handle. It was failure to install control systems of the type required by the size of the business and the need for a more human face in labour relations that were the main ingredients in Ford's decline.

It is romanticism, not objective analysis, that attributes survival motives to the technostructure of the mature corporation and entre-preneurial characteristics only to the smaller units in the economy. The compulsions of modern technology are such that many schemes can only be undertaken by financially strong corporations. Is the Brunei/Japan liquefied natural gas project, which pushed technology forward in several directions, to be dubbed a pedestrian product of mature corp-orations because it costs a few hundred million pounds? Is it not just possible that some of the mature corporations in the North Sea are show-ing a few signs of entrepreneurship?

V. Profits, Prices and Planners

There is a great deal of nonsense written and talked about risk taking and investment—the bulk of it by people who have never made a major investment decision in their lives. In the United Kingdom hardly a week passes without Mr Jack Jones[1] intoning his left-wing liturgy that there has been an investment strike by private enterprise. Like Galbraith he feels it quite unnecessary to produce any proof of his assertions; it is sufficient that he says it. Or perhaps he relies on the Government White Paper *The Regeneration of British Industry* where we read "In 1971, investment for each worker in British manufacturing industry was less than half that in France, Japan or the United States and well below that in Germany or Italy".[2] Here again there is no factual analysis; nor is any attempt made to find an answer to the problem other than lack of investment. Yet if you build a modern steel plant or invest in a modern ship-building facility and employ twice the manpower that our main competitors find necessary, it is obvious that the capital invested per worker will be halved. Here the fault does not lie in lack of investment; the overmanning and under-utilization of existing plant and equipment is both a contributor to Britain's current malaise and a major inhibitor of investment in modern machinery. Many working men are well aware of this even if some of their trades unions and the political dependents of the unions prefer to observe a conspiracy of silence.

It is also misleading to talk about investment in general terms as if it were somehow homogeneous; it is not. Some investments—pollution control and safety at work for example—are often legally required and do not permit of profit or pay-out analysis. But the bulk of investment is incurred to meet either a new or increased demand or an existing demand in a less costly fashion or a combination of both. Whatever the motivation, capital expenditure is always made in terms of specific plant, property and equipment. It is usually implemented when forward estimates show the probability of a better return on capital than any alter-

21

native use of the resources. However, in spite of Galbraith and the much more constructive efforts of the Harvard Business School, it is still impossible to assess future profitability in any exact manner. True, a cost saving investment—such as moving oil in a 300,000 ton tanker rather than six 50,000 tonners—can be calculated with a fair degree of accuracy. But all investments—and this irrespective of how refined we make the calculations of present-day value, earning power and pay-out time—finally involve an act of judgment or an act of faith. Nobody can foretell the future with sufficient accuracy to remove the uncertainty inherent in its unfolding.

When Messrs Jones and Varley[3] lecture the rest of us in Britain about the need to increase investment they cannot surely mean that we should do so unselectively.[4] With a 1976 estimated industry requirement of approximately 240m tons deadweight of oil tankers and an availability of over 325m tons, they would not presumably advocate investing in more ultra large or very large crude oil carriers; nor, presumably, should there be more investment in crude oil distillation capacity when, outside the USA, those already built are operating at something like 70 per cent of capacity. If their words have any meaning at all, it can only be that in their opinion the multiplicity of individuals and companies who make investment decisions are taking too gloomy a view of the economy and the future profitability of their industries. This could well be true. But sight should not be lost of the fact that the people making investment decisions usually have to live with the consequences of these decisions; the advice-givers are not so handicapped. It should also be remembered that it is inherent in the nature of business that some investment decisions will prove wrong. When the decision making process is fairly widely dispersed errors will, to some extent, cancel each other out. But when decisions are made on a monolithic basis, errors—and errors there will be—are bound to be monolithic also. It is quite legitimate therefore to examine the credentials of those who are giving advice so lavishly and who, in so doing, are trying to replace the dispersed judgments of the many by the assessments of the few—an aim which also represents the culmination of Galbraith's philosophy.

Here there is little ground for confidence. The people who advance the somewhat arrogant claim to superiority are the same people who have subjected the United Kingdom to what John Jewkes so aptly termed successive "ordeals by planning". They are much the same people who assured us in 1965 that we were "on our way" to a 3.8 per cent per annum compound growth rate propelled by a "new machine" in the shape of the national plan. The designers of the new machine had not the remotest idea of what type of fuel would keep the Daedalian monster in motion. Not that this mattered too much; it collapsed even before anyone could find the starting handle.[5] They are the same people who have permitted public expenditure over substantial areas to run out of control and who have debauched the currency on a scale never before witnessed in the history of Britain. They are the same people who, at a meeting of the National Economic Development Council in 1976, rejected as utterly unacceptable the Treasury's lower estimate of economic growth, apparently on the ground that a higher rate would be necessary to make any sense out of even the reduced level of government expenditure.[6] How the higher rate was to be achieved remained wrapped in mystery.

Organizations do not behave responsibly when they try to handle problems outside their sphere of competence. The views of the Royal Society for the Prevention of Cruelty to Animals should command respect on all aspects of animal welfare; their views on the relative merits of fixed or floating exchange rates are of little relevance. Yet some trade unionists, politicians and bureaucrats appear to think, with Galbraith, that their sphere of competence knows no bounds. Thus Mr Jack Jones has become an authority on almost every subject from the value of the Victoria Cross to Ascot races, from monetary policy and defence to education. The wider his canvas, the more *ex cathedra* become his pronouncements. Again, the more governments overload themselves with problems that they have neither the training nor the experience to handle, the less well do they discharge their traditional functions. This is becoming painfully clear in Britain in spite of the undoubted ability of most of its senior civil servants. An aggravating factor is that ministers are often moved around with a rapidity that precludes their acquiring a basic knowledge or expertise on the subjects with which they are supposed to deal. Yet there are signs that people are becoming a little tired of the sick, slick, gimmicky cleverness of the last decade and would prefer a little more wisdom in the economic sphere. It certainly would mark a considerable advance if, to parody Ellis Parker Butler, cows of all breeds could be induced to abandon their more frivolous pursuits such as jumping over the moon and made instead to focus their attention on simple milk-producing activities like eating grass and chewing the cud. If this means that most of the academic economists who clutter the corridors of power should revert to their traditional role of teaching the young, so be it. Great achievements usually involve some sacrifice; this is one the country could well afford.

Galbraith derides the description of the American economy as a profit and loss system--the hope of profit being the incentive and the fear of loss being the spur—on the grounds that mature corporations can protect their profits by planning and that U.S. Steel has not made a loss for twenty-five years. Galbraith's argument about U.S. Steel must mean that unless each and every company suffers a loss at some period in its history the economy cannot be described as being subjected to the profit and loss discipline. This is indeed a strange process of reasoning. It would seem a tenable proposition to state that a master mariner's desire to retain command and his pride in running a good ship are the incentives while fear of stranding it is the spur. Not so, would say Galbraith, since the vast majority of captains achieve retirement age without stranding a single ship and most vessels reach their final ignominy in the breaker's yard without having hit bottom once. Again, it would seem quite reasonable to say that the joy of living acts as an incentive to good driving on the road; the fear of death or mutilation is the spur. Not so, would say Galbraith, in the forty years the author of that remark has been driving he has not been killed or mutilated once. But being killed or mutilated usually happens only once. It is not necessary for an underlying risk to materialize on each and every occasion to make it a spur; the fact that it could happen is usually sufficient.

The same is true of business. People create their firms, maintain and develop them, whether as individuals or members of a technostructure, with a view to making a profit. Once a company ceases to make a profit, or even where the return on capital employed is inadequate, it leaves itself open to takeover or, eventually, liquidation. However, there are some exceptions to this in Britain. Here the overall economy is being pulled down by the apparent acceptance of the principle that, in certain areas, a worker has the right to retain for his working life the same job at the same place at wages in no way related to the value of his output. Government sometimes likes to give the impression that it has a widow's cruse which makes the financing of its expenditure painless. This is not so: the rest of the community as taxpayers or, more viciously, the victims of inflation have to meet these costs. It is difficult to see how a dynamic economy can be created, either with or without the "white heat of the modern scientific revolution," when, as in Britain, success is so heavily penalized to subsidize failure.[7]

Galbraith asserts that control of prices in the planning sector is not a problem. He maintains that the mature corporation can protect its profits by planning and that the technostructure aims to make a level of profits which will achieve the twofold objective of preventing the shareholders from interfering and insulating it from the capital market. From those propositions it would appear that the technostructure has both the power and the motivation to make profits increase by at least a modest amount each year. Yet let us examine first how this has worked out in the real world by considering the Royal Dutch/Shell Group.

It had its origins in the nineteenth century; by 1975 its gross revenues were £18,870m, or £15,189m if sales tax, excise duties and similar levies are excluded; group net assets at the end of 1975 were £5,775m; its employees totalled 161,000. As there can be little doubt that it falls into the planning system its technostructure should, therefore, wield the powers that Galbraith ascribes to it. Table 1 shows the net income (excluding changes due to conversion of foreign currencies) of the Royal Dutch/Shell Group for the ten years to 1975.

TABLE 1

	1966	1967	1968	1969	1970	1971	1972	1973	1974	1975
Net Income (£m)	236	270	389	420	391	375	221	702	1093	950
Pence per Imp. Gall.	0.45	0.46	0.61	0.59	0.49	0.47	0.32	0.76	1.38	1.24
% of Average Net Assets	8.4	9.2	12.1	12.4	10.9	9.9	5.6	16.9	22.8	17.4
% of Average Net Assets on a C.P.P. basis	—	—	—	—	—	—	—	—	10.9	2.7

The net income is shown in terms of (a) absolute amounts, (b) pence per imperial gallon of sales, (c) as a percentage of average net assets, and (d) as a percentage of average net assets on a current purchasing power basis. The last is put in for the years 1974 and 1975 to highlight the ravages of inflation. From this table it will be noted that from 1969 to 1972 net profit fell from £420m to £221m; expressed in pence per imperial gallon it tumbled from 0.59 to 0.32, while in terms of return on net assets it dropped from 12.4 per cent to 5.6 per cent. From the figures it will be seen that it only required an increase of a small fraction of a penny per gallon during the declining years to reverse the trend and keep the profit on a steady upward course.

Now the Shell planners were not emulating the Sleeping Beauty at this particular juncture in history; indeed it was one of their more prolific periods. The fact was that, in the markets in which Shell operated, the competitive position did not permit of higher prices or lower costs and there were no means whereby the Group could insulate itself from these forces. Galbraith's matter of no difficulty—increasing prices —proved in practice to be an insurmountable obstacle.[8] Other companies have sometimes fared much worse than Shell. For example, in 1975, 16 per cent of the 500 largest companies outside the USA disclosed losses totalling approximately US $3,800m—a fitting epitaph rather than an *encomium* on the conceivable omnipotence of the technostructure.

As already stated, Galbraith relies heavily on the automobile industry to justify his assertions. Let us therefore look at the profit record of the four main American producers for the period 1966-1975.

TABLE 2

Net Income (Loss) in US$ million

	1966	1967	1968	1969	1970	1971	1972	1973	1974	1975
General Motors	1793	1627	1732	1711	609	1936	2163	2398	950	1253
Ford	621	184	627	547	516	657	870	907	361	323
Chrysler	194	203	303	99	(8)	84	220	255	(52)	(260)
American Motors	(13)	(76)	12	5	56	10	30	86	28	(28)

There is nothing in these figures to give any comfort or support to Galbraith's argument. If the technostructure, or planners, of General Motors really possessed the "conceivably omnipotent" or "plenary" powers he ascribes to them, why did they permit the net income in 1970 to fall to 34 per cent of what it was in 1966 and were they happy to see a net income in 1975 only 70 per cent of what it had been a decade previously? Surely, had the power really existed, it would have been used to arrest the decline.

Nor is there anything in the experience of the British motor industry to substantiate Galbraith's analysis. In the early 1960s Britain ranked second in the world league table of motor car producers; by the mid-1970s it has been surpassed by West Germany, France, Italy and Japan. In the early 1960s it produced about a quarter of the cars manufactured outside North America; by the mid-1970s its share had shrunk to one tenth. In the early 1960s imported cars accounted for one-twentieth of new registrations; by the mid-1970s they were just short of one-third. Profit performance, which in Galbraithian terms is easily arranged by the technostructure, was erratic. British Leyland, for example, went from a profit of £19m in 1968 to a loss of £6m in 1970; it recovered to a profit of £23m in the following year. By 1975 it had joined the 'lame ducks' seeking government aid, to be followed a little later by Chrysler (UK) Limited. If the technostructure exercised the powers attributed to it by Galbraith the deterioration would never have been allowed to occur, particularly as the 'survival' of several of its members was at stake. The blunt fact is that these powers only exist in the fantasy world of John Kenneth Galbraith.

Neither does the idea that the technostructure wishes to avoid the capital market so as to preserve its autonomy stand up to critical analysis. Managements generally know that investment in new projects cannot exceed the money that can be generated by depreciation, ploughed-back profits and the amount that can be raised in the capital markets either by new equity issues or borrowing. True, there can be differing views of the gearing appropriate to a particular industry or a particular company. But to state that one of the aims of the technostructure is to try to avoid the capital market because it involves establishing the credit worthiness of the company is simply not true. Of course, the managements of some companies may wish to avoid too deep an investigation into their affairs; but these are in the minority. More are jealous of their credit rating and take steps to maintain and improve it. When the Royal Dutch/Shell Group had its Triple A rating reaffirmed by the two United States rating agencies in 1976, members of its finance department were aglow, not with indignation at the interference in their autonomy through the necessary probing, but because the Group they represented enjoyed the highest possible credit rating.

At the end of 1975 the long-term debt of the Royal Dutch/Shell Group was £1,936m; that of General Motors was US $1,223m; Chrysler Corporation US $1,067m; United Technologies US $637m; and McDonnell Douglas US $246m. Redemption and refunding of debt on this scale is a continuous process. It would be irresponsible to inhibit the growth of a corporation by regarding incursions into the capital market as interfering with the autonomy of the technostructure. Apart from Galbraith there may be the odd eccentric in a corporation who, for religious or resistance to interference motives, refuses to borrow; a perusal of the balance sheets of Fortune's five hundred corporations will show that he is not really a dominant force in any of them.

When Galbraith expounds his views about the role of planners, he tacitly assumes that the mature corporations rely only on the market sector for their supplies. He gives a David and Goliath flavour to the new industrial state with Goliath naturally grinding little David's face into the profitless dust. Yet if, perchance, little David has a patent for a coating which helps to prevent cracking in the fan blades of a turbine engine, he has, in proportion to his size, much more market power than

27

General Motors—at least until some credible alternative appears. True, as Galbraith says, little David may be dependent on engine manufacturers and the big airlines for his outlet. The big airlines, however, have an acute need for little David's product and such little Davids often make returns on their capital that are the envy of some of the mature corporations they supply. As already stated, it is not size but availability of alternatives that is the main criterion of market power. Again, in the North Sea there are consortia composed of relatively small companies and some of the largest mature corporations in the world. There is no evidence to support the view that the latter have been able to compel suppliers to provide equipment at the prices they determine.

TABLE 3
Progression of Steel Platform Costs 1970-75
Cost by year at current prices: (£m.)

Cost category	1970	1971	1972	1973	1974	1975
Management	3.9	4.7	5.3	6.0	6.9	8.3
Design effort	2.6	3.1	3.5	3.9	4.4	5.6
Steel	3.3	3.9	4.2	4.2	6.5	8.1
Jacket fabrication	21.2	24.6	27.5	38.1	44.4	55.0
Manufactured equipment	20.1	22.1	23.5	25.3	29.4	36.2
Module fabrication	3.7	4.1	4.6	5.3	6.2	8.0
Offshore services	1.4	1.6	1.9	2.4	3.2	4.0
Offshore transport	1.8	2.0	2.1	2.3	2.7	3.5
Offshore installation	8.4	10.8	13.3	16.6	24.3	26.5
Total	66.4	76.9	85.9	104.1	128.0	155.2
Index of costs	100	116	129	157	193	224

Table 3 taken from a study by the UK Government on North Sea cost escalation shows that the cost of an offshore steel platform escalated by just under two and a half times between 1970 and 1975. These cost increases affected all operators—Goliaths as well as Davids, the planning system as well as the market sector.

Moreover, mature corporations do not only deal with the market sector; they trade with each other on a large scale. Here Galbraith's analysis runs into more difficulties. What happens when the conceivably omnipotent planners in Shell, leaning forward to compel customers to take aviation turbine fuel at the price they dictate, are confronted with

28

British Airways' planners, themselves armed with plenary powers to compel their suppliers to provide aviation turbine fuel at the price they have determined? Ringside seats should command a premium; the scene has all the potential of the trial by combat between King Arthur and the Roman tribune Flollo.

> Taking their stand opposite each other and couching lance in rest, they forthwith set spurs to their steeds and smote together with a right mighty shock. But Arthur, who bore his spear the more heedfully, thrust the same into the top of Flollo's breast and, shielding off the other's blow with all the force he might, bore him to the ground. Then, unsheathing his sword, he was hastening to smite him, when Flollo, on his legs in an instant, ran upon him with his spear levelled, and with deadly thrust into his destrier's chest, brought both horse and rider to the ground. The fight continued afoot until Arthur, excited by the sight of his own outpouring blood, gave his opponent the final stroke. Flollo fell and beating the ground with his heels, gave up his ghost to the winds.[10]

This mediaeval example of monopolistic competition *a outrance* may have a place in Galbraith's unreal world of convoluted power, but it has no place in the true industrial state. It would soon run out of planners if it did. In the example given, the normal procedure would be for the airline to negotiate with its suppliers or call for tenders. Since by the nature of the airline industry suppliers are needed at many airfields, quotations are often required for each delivery point. The oil companies selling the turbine fuel have varying costs at the different supply points. A large refinery near an airfield will give a cost advantage over a competitor whose supply source involves transporting turbine fuel over a long distance on a small product tanker. The market for gasoline and domestic kerosine in Singapore and Indonesia, for example, may be buoyant and this would tend to set a floor price for aviation turbine fuel in that area. Yet even here the supplier might, for any one of a number of reasons, quote a finer price than the immediate market situation would justify: there may be future uncertainties, on both volume and price, in the spot market; there may be a desire to maintain a foothold in what could be a rapidly expanding market; or there may be a need for an acceptable level of throughput at an existing airport facility. On the side of the airline, factors such as substantial reciprocal business, prompt service that helps speed the turn-round time of aeroplanes, and reliability of supply in time of crisis could well make them concede a slightly higher price to a good proven operator. Subject to these relatively minor qualifications contracts will normally be awarded on the basis of the lowest price for the same quality product at each main delivery point. The profitability of the transactions to the oil companies will vary according to their costs and market conditions. When supplies are tight the price and the profit per unit are likely to be higher than when the market is sloppy. In other words the price will reflect the underlying factors of supply and demand. This may all seem rather dull and pedestrian, lacking as it does the great potential for fun presented by Galbraith's analysis. Alas, this is the price reality sometimes has to pay to put a romancer into perspective.[11]

It is often assumed that the degree of competition and prices in a particular market are a function of the number of producers and consumers involved. This can be a factor, but the pressure of total demand on total supply availability is more important than the actual number of operators on either side of the equation. When total demand presses hard on total supply availability, prices rise, delivery dates are lengthened and those first in the queue, if they have assignable contracts, can usually sell their positions at a substantial profit if they calculate this to be to their financial advantage. This was the position in the shipbuilding boom which followed the scramble to build the very economic large crude oil carriers and in the first stages of airline re-equipment with wide-bodied subsonic jets. When the tanker market ran into surplus and the re-equipment of the airlines, admittedly at a lower level of demand due to the world recession, was nearing completion the position was reversed. Prices were brought closer to costs, and in some instances probably below cost, to keep skilled labour forces together; delivery dates shortened. As a result of the latter, buyers regarded the pressure to order well ahead to meet their requirements as having been reduced; they could afford to wait before placing orders to see if demand was really developing according to their estimates.

A recent review of British Airways' long-haul market indicated that probably about 15 per cent of it could be met most economically by Tri-Star jets with a lower capacity than the various versions of the Boeing 747 Jumbo. There were only really two competitors in this field—Lockheed and McDonnell Douglas. Lockheed saw it as a logical extension into a long-range version thereby ensuring some continuity in its civil aviation business. McDonnell Douglas saw a Rolls Royce engined version of its DC-10 as increasing the market potential for an already successful aircraft. Had the prices of both the tri-jets been excessive there would have been crossover points in favour of various combinations of additional Boeing 747s, and some of the narrow bodied jets in service. In practice, the desire of both main contenders for the tri-jet order was so great that it is doubtful if competition on price and delivery dates could have been keener had there been fifteen, instead of two, producers. This is not a plea for fewer producers—far from it; it is a plea not to exaggerate the powers wielded in situations of duopoly or oligopoly when the compulsions of technology press a complex product in the direction of a smaller number of production units.

Galbraith contends that a mature corporation can insulate itself from market forces by integrating its operations from the raw material to the final consumer. Within limits this is true. There is, however, no large corporation that is completely integrated in the sense that it buys nothing in the market place; indeed, to endeavour to do so would pose many problems. Dunlop, or any other tyre manufacturer, might well buy, as they have done, a rubber estate to provide one of its most important raw materials. But the operation of a rubber estate requires fertilisers, tapping knives, coagulating acid, chengkuls, motor transport and a host of other equipment. These are bought in the market place. It would be silly and uneconomic for any company to try to produce all these things itself. It also has to hire transportation space by rail, road and sea to the point of manufacture where numerous other items, canvas, carbon black and so forth, have to be purchased in the market place before the final product can be manufactured. Even so, it can be argued that by investing in a rubber estate the tyre manufacturer has insulated himself to a marked degree from fluctuations in the price of natural rubber. Whether this gives an advantage over a competitor who is content to buy rubber on the market on the various contractual terms available, however, depends on the return made on the investment. If, over a period, natural rubber prices remain so high that the return on capital employed is appreciably above that shown by an investment in actual tyre manufacturing, the estate-owner will have gained an advantage over his competitor. The reverse will be true if the plantation investment shows a relatively lower return.

Likewise, an oil company, in purchasing or chartering tankers, insulates itself from fluctuations in market rates. Whether or not this produces an advantage depends on the relationship between its costs on its committed fleet and future movements in charter rates. Those oil companies which had covered their requirements prior to the various Suez crises, when rates moved sharply upwards, were at a considerable advantage over those who had played the market short. Conversely any company which covered itself in advance for its current (1976) operations would be at a severe disadvantage in comparison with its less covered competitors whose shortfall could be made up at freight rates that barely cover the direct operating costs of the vessels. Integration is not an unmixed blessing: it insulates its practitioners from the market place but can produce severe disadvantages. It certainly does not enhance the power of the technostructure in the manner suggested by Galbraith.

Incidentally, the obverse of the oil companies' problem is to be found with the independent tanker owners. If vessels are let on long-term charter which covers a crisis period, the return on capital will for a time be smaller, sometimes very substantially smaller, than the owner who operates the spot market. The reverse is now true with the current collapse of freight rates; tanker owners without long-term charters are in grave financial difficulties. All of them had made their assessments of the future; some were content with a relatively small return but with the security of a long-term charter; others preferred to take the "boom and bust" risks of the spot market; some did both to varying degrees. The bulk of them were entrepreneurial corporations on Galbraith's definition; they approached the market in a widely different fashion. The economy does not fit into neat stereotyped slots.

Notes

1. General Secretary, Transport and General Workers Union.
2. Cmnd. 5710, p. 1, HMSO, 1974.
3. Secretary of State for Industry.
4. *1977 Economic Review,* TUC, 1976; National Economic Development Council Meetings, July & August, 1976.
5. John Brunner, *The National Plan: A Preliminary Assessment,* Institute of Economic Affairs, 1965 (3rd edition, 1969).
6. 'Wishing won't make it so', Leader in *The Times,* 6 August, 1976.
7. G.C. Allen, *The British Disease,* Institute of Economic Affairs, 1976.
8. Sir Frank McFadzean, *Galbraith and the Planners,* Strathclyde University Press, 1968.
9. *The Future of the British Car Industry,* Central Policy Review Staff, HMSO, 1975; Sir Don Ryder, *British Leyland: the next decade,* HMSO, 1975; *The British Motor Vehicle Industry,* Cmnd. 6377, HMSO, 1976.
10. Elizabeth Jenkins, *The Mystery of King Arthur,* Joseph, 1975.
11. Armen A. Alchien, *Pricing and Society,* Institute of Economic Affairs, 1967.

VI. Eliminating Uncertainty

One of the major aims of the corporate planner, says Galbraith, is the elimination of uncertainty. Those of us who have managed large corporations have not yet been able to identify anyone with this talent; and if genetic engineers ever succeed in creating him, it is unlikely that he will be found plodding up the career ladder in the technostructure of a mature corporation. A talent for eliminating uncertainty would be more remunerative and satisfying than owning a licence to print money. After all, the latter injures your fellow man and eventually finishes in a blind alley when the cost of paper exceeds the largest value note that the public is prepared to accept. The former suffers from no such inhibitions. If, in eliminating uncertainty, this yet to be created genius makes millions of dollars for himself and his friends he should not find his success burdened with any sense of guilt. In eliminating uncertainty for himself he will almost certainly have reduced it for others. A state of supreme bliss for the timid will be that much closer.

Some of the potential for a would-be eliminator of uncertainty can be gauged by glancing at Table 4 over.

This table was compiled on 27 August 1976 and shows for a few commodities the current price, the price on the corresponding date a year previously, the highest and lowest prices for the current year and the percentage variation of the high from the low. All these commodities fluctuate daily when the markets are open. In the first eight months of 1976 prices moved quite widely for every commodity shown; the variation between low and high was smallest in the case of linseed oil at 21 per cent, and highest in the case of coffee at 115 per cent. But—and this is the main point when the supposed powers of economic planners are under consideration—if anyone had been able in January 1976 to forecast the price movements of any one of the commodities on the list, and had been prepared to back his forecast, he could have made himself rich beyond the dreams of avarice. Nobody was able to do so.

TABLE 4

Prices per Ton (unless otherwise stated)

	27th Aug. 1976	Year Previous	1976 High	1976 Low	Difference expressed as a % of low
Metals					
Aluminium	£527	£396	£527	£420	25
Antimony	£2,150	£1,450	£2,150	£1,450	48
Copper (Cash Wire Bars)	£859	£626	£937	£575	63
Lead	£275	£185	£291	£163	78
Gold (per oz.)	$ 104	$162	$141	$104	36
Tin	£4,503	£3,198	£4,893	£3,057	60
Grains					
Barley	£77	£63	£77	£63	22
Wheat (Eng. milling)	£85	£65	£85	£66	29
Vegetable Oils					
Groundnut	£427	£462	£461	£372	23
Linseed	£458	£463	£458	£377	21
Other Commodities					
Cocoa	£1,427	£598	£1,459	£725	101
Coffee (Future 2nd pos.)	£1,555	£776	£1,696	£787	115
Rubber (kilo)	49p	36p	55p	37p	49
Sugar (raw)	£127	£200	£205	£123	67

Yet if planners—or anybody else for that matter—are unable to forecast accurately what is, after all, but a tiny segment of the economy, how can they foresee the vast range and variety of risks which, according to Galbraith, they are supposed to be eliminating? True, most commodity markets have facilities for hedging risks but, like the tanker example already noted, it only gives an assurance about the future costs of the company doing the hedging. Whether this will prove beneficial or not depends on how spot prices move and the degree to which its competitors are similarly covered.

Corporate planners do not usually view their function in the grandiloquent terms used by Galbraith; they know full well that the elimination of uncertainty is not of this world, nor of Galbraith's world—if it ever comes. Uncertainties stem from many sources; we have already touched upon those inherent in the market place. But the last decade or so the most important and most de-stabilising, from a business point of view, have been political in their origin. Let me highlight a few from a long and dreary catalogue. The fourfold increase in the price of oil in a short period of time, with its dramatic effect on the balance of payments of consuming countries and its contribution to recession, was the act of an inter-governmental cartel.[1] The nationalization of industries at net book value—vicious enough in times of currency stability, confiscatory in times of inflation—or at stock exchange prices themselves driven down by the shrill threats of the left (intent, as the late Anthony Crosland once put it, in dragging Marks and Spencer up to the high level of efficiency of the Co-op)[2]—was political in origin and bound to inhibit investment. So too were the uncertainties engendered by inflationary monetary and fiscal policies, particularly in the United Kingdom where even a Conservative prime minister misled himself into believing that deep-seated social attitudes could be changed by monetary gimmickry—a disaster continued with much greater vigour by the succeeding Labour administrations until sterling had fallen, on a trade-weighted basis, by approximately 44 per cent from the time of the Smithsonian currency agreement to the end of 1976. Price controls, wage controls, and labour and tax legislation in such profusion that even law-abiding citizens are no longer sure about the legality of some of their actions have all been instigated by politicians and have all added to the great tide of uncertainty. The vagaries of the market are much more easily handled than the vagaries of interventionist politicians who are far from being as ideally wise or benevolent as most of them would have the rest of us believe.[3] Adam Smith's contemporary and friend, Edmund Burke, displayed a fine contempt for these zealots of regulation. When they deploy their "coercive guidance" to interfere with the adjustments of supply and demand said Burke, "all the principles of the market will be subverted; a monopoly of authority in the market will ruin whatever it touches".[4]

Uncertainties can also stem from purely physical factors. Crop failures in Russia—a fairly regular occurence—can result in large demands being placed on the grain availabilities in other countries such as the USA, Canada and Australia. This has repercussions not only on the balances of payments of the countries concerned, but also on the freight rates in both the dry cargo and tanker markets. The difference between a mild and a very cold winter in Western Europe can make a difference in demand of several million tons of oil not only for direct home heating but also for electricity generation.

Uncertainties also arise from technological advances. Large and expensive units of equipment like tankers, distillation columns, ethylene crackers and so forth usually have physical lives of around twenty years or more during which period there will obviously be advances that cannot at present be foreseen. How, within the limits of our present knowledge, does one gauge whether any probable improvement in technology will render an investment in such equipment economically obsolescent before the end of its life or, even more important, before the capital expenditure has been recovered? For example, a liquefied natural gas tanker carries its cargo at a temperature of minus 161°C. As the steel plate used in ordinary ship construction turns brittle at this temperature heavy insulation has to be built between the outer hull and the cargo. A technical breakthrough would considerably lessen the cost of constructing this specialized form of transport. All such possibilities have to be continuously assessed if a corporation is not to be burdened by higher unit costs than its competitors. However, the heavy inflation rates of the last few years have helped to salvage errors of judgment in this particular area.

Of course it can be argued that corporate planners aim at reducing—I have never heard any of them use the word eliminating—uncertainty and, to some extent, they succeed. Yet the residual area of uncertainty is so great that if this were to be the criterion for judging planners it would be necessary to regard them as failures. To take a practical example, the Royal Dutch/Shell Group's actual performance in 1975 was recently compared with the estimate made in 1971 of what it would be four years later. Volumetrically the forecast sales of oil outside North America were approximately 7m barrels per day; actual sales were 4.2m barrels a day. Refinery capacity forecast requirements, again outside North America, were around 6m barrels a day in terms of primary distillation capacity; actual crude oil intake was 2.6m barrels a day. Tanker requirements were estimated at 2,474 T2 equivalents; the actual programme required 1,241 T2 equivalents. Costs per unit of sales were estimated to be just over $3.30; actual costs were $14.12. Proceeds per unit of sales were estimated to be about $4 per barrel; the figure actually realized was just under $14.90.

This example has been given not to suggest that Shell planners are stupid. This is far from being so and there is certainly no reason to believe that their performance, given the ambient circumstances of OPEC and economic recession, was in any way inferior to that of planners in other corporations. It has been given to highlight the limitations of all planning and to underline that its practitioners do not possess the great powers attributed to them by Galbraith. Of course the changed circumstances of 1975 compared with what had been forecast in 1971 did not come upon the planners with cataclysmic suddenness. By 1972 and 1973 it had become clear that the volume and price assumptions for 1975 were no longer tenable. In just under two years OPEC pushed producer government revenue per barrel of oil from \$1.43 to \$9.23 in terms of the marker crude (Arabian Light 34^0). However, de-gearing an organization to meet such dramatically changed circumstances poses many problems. For example, the long lead-in time between signature of contracts and the completion of a refinery or a large tanker, particularly when builders are overloaded as they were in the early 1970s, severely circumscribes the room for manoeuvre. It was, for example, obvious by 1973/4 that there was going to be a substantial surplus of both refineries and tankers but the costs of cancellations were, in many cases, so high that it paid to continue the contracts even although this involved mothballing or laying up on completion. In the case of tankers, industry requirements by the end of 1974 were $\pm$ 209m tonnes, while availability at $\pm$ 253 million tonnes was over 20 per cent higher. In spite of this surplus, and an estimated continuing decline in demand, the year 1975 saw an addition of 44m tonnes of new buildings to the world's fleets. By the end of the year the surplus had grown to approximately 50 per cent above requirements. Although every effort was made to dissipate this surplus by chartering out into the ore and grain trades, accelerated scrapping, economic and deep slow steaming and use of ships as floating storage, approximately 47m tons of mainly very large crude carriers were in lay-up by the end of 1975. Several of them belonged to mature corporations. There was nothing the planners could do about it. They had to bow to market conditions.

There is some force in the argument that the examples given are not really representative; they cover a period of time when there were two major discontinuities which would not be typical of the normal planning process over a longer time span. Yet any distortion from the norm relates less to the existence of the errors than their magnitude. Even if the two major discontinuities had not arisen it would be wrong to believe that the planners would have been on target. Indeed, a check on the forward estimates made in the 1960s against the subsequent realities disclosed that throughout the period there were appreciable variations in volumes, costs and prices due to changes in market circumstances. There were always some discontinuities unforeseen when the plans were initiated. Nor were these problems peculiar to the oil industry. Although of a different order of magnitude the planners involved in electricity generation and world airlines, to mention only two other industries, faced similar difficulties of adjusting to much lower demand levels than had been forecast.

The object of corporate planning is much more modest than the role ascribed to it by Galbraith. At any particular moment in time a corporation is confronted with a given factual position: it is a prisoner of its past decisions (which may or may not have been correct—they seldom are with hindsight) on personnel, marketing and investment policies. Starting from this base the planners try to assess future developments as they affect the corporation's interests. Galbraith's attempt to portray the planners of General Motors—or Shell or British Airways—as approaching their task by determining first the profit they wish to earn, secondly what they are going to produce and, thirdly, how to foist their production on the consumer is the reverse of the truth. Most planning starts off in the market place with research into customer requirements and the probable future trend of their preferences; it involves assessments of the probable total market, the strengths, weaknesses and probable intentions of competitors; it involves assessing the probable trend of the corporation's own volume of products, probable prices and costs; it involves assessing the probable generation of funds and the amounts available for investment; it involves assessing changes in technology and the additional investments necessary to meet the projected demand at the lowest possible costs; it involves assessing the political climate in which business will be allowed to operate. The ultimate objective is to try to arrange the affairs of the enterprise so as to produce the maximum return on its investments. This is not always achieved in practice but the aim remains.[5] If any Shell manager—and the same is probably true of most, if not all, mature corporations—advanced his forward plans on the basis that they were designed to ensure his survival and that of his colleagues, to earn sufficient profit to keep the shareholders quiet and avoid the treasurer's department having to raise funds in the market, he would be regarded by his colleagues as having taken leave of his senses. His future career would depend on an assessment of whether his mind was overthrown on a temporary or permanent basis.

But were he to add that he exercised powers which were plenary in their nature and, therefore, made him omnipotent, it would be obvious that no amount of flangeing up could restore his unhinged mind to normal functioning.

Most members of the technostructure of large corporations would welcome constructive criticism of the manner in which they discharge their functions; in most organizations there is scope for improvement. But this is not what Galbraith sets out to do. Without any supporting evidence he expects his readers to accept that descriptions of motivation and behaviour, which provoke surprise and derision among those who actually manage large corporations, are nevertheless a true mirror of the underlying reality. It is a lot to expect.

Notes

1. Colin Robinson, *The Energy 'Crisis' and British Coal,* Institute of Economic Affairs, 1975.
2. Richard Evans, 'Social democracy's gifted theorist', *Financial Times,* 21 February 1977.
3. Gordon Tullock, *The Vote Motive,* Institute of Economic Affairs, 1976.
4. 'Thoughts and Details upon Scarcity', *The Works of the Right Honourable Edmund Burke,* Vol. VII, C. & J. Rivington, 1826.
5. Sir Frank McFadzean, *Galbraith and the Planners,* Strathclyde University Press, 1968.

VII. Public Cognizance

Galbraith is a skilful and amusing fabricator of phrases; he obviously delights in the use of exotic language. In Chapter XXIV of *Economics and the Public Purpose* we are introduced to what is grandly called the "emancipation of the State from the planning system". He manufactures the phrase "public cognizance" to describe the political recognition of a divergence between the aims and objects of the planning system of large corporations and what he classifies as the public interest. Having thus created an area of potential conflict he throws the issue into confusion by blithely asserting that, in the USA, the relations between large corporations and the government are symbiotic in nature. Symbiotic and symbiosis appear so many times in his book that they must now be regarded as being among the 'in' words with phrases like "techno-structure" and "private affluence and public squalor". Having heard symbiotic used before only to describe the relationship between certain types of ants and aphids which, as a by-product of their intimacy, spread bunchy top disease in the hemp plantations of North Borneo, it was necessary for me to resort to the dictionary. The *Concise Oxford* confirmed that symbiosis is the permanent union between organisms "each of which depends for its existence on the other as the fungus and alga in lichen"; *Chambers Dictionary* likewise informs us that it is "a mutually beneficial partnership between organisms of different kinds". Put another way, the essence of symbiosis is to be found in that charming Indonesian phrase *gotong rojong* which was popularised by another famous juggler of words—the late President Sukarno. The meaning of *gotong rojong* is mutual assistance or inter-dependence—each side helps the other, neither side dominates. Galbraith cannot have it both ways. If, as he asserts, government "has to be broken free from the *control* of the planning system", the relationship between the two can hardly be classified as symbiotic.

Galbraith creates an atmosphere of suspicion around the close relationship that undoubtedly exists in the USA between government and the defence industries. But this is surely the result of the compulsions of technology which he stresses so much. The growing complexity and cost of weapons systems have resulted in increased concentration in the industries supplying the sophisticated hardware. It has also created a wider and deeper interface between suppliers and the defence procurement agencies. That such relationships can have dangers is undoubtedly true, but it is stretching imagination too far to describe it in terms of a battle for domination between the government and the corporation concerned. The participants do not view it in this light.

Galbraith also reads a lot into the fact that the chairman of General Motors from time to time meets the President of the United States of America. Whether or not he has a prescriptive right to do so on every visit to Washington—as Galbraith suggests—I am in no position to judge; yet there seems to be nothing abnormal about the head of a large organization having an exchange of views with a President or Prime Minister. True, if politicians having been playing havoc in the market place there could well be differences to be discussed and, if possible, resolved. But such occasions, although growing, are probably exceptional and most differences of this kind will usually be resolved at a lower level. Many more intelligent politicians—and this applies in virtually all countries— like to be informed of industrial matters at first hand; it is therefore silly to interpret such visits in terms of power struggles. Yet they obviously irritate Galbraith mightily—possibly due to an underlying frustration that so much can take place in the corridors of power without his personal involvement.

Even in a book resplendent in unsupported generalizations, some of the assertions in the last few chapters of *Economics and the Public Purpose* are quite breathtaking. Like some latter day economic Bourbon he seems to have learned nothing from the recent experience of Britain and other countries; and he seems to have forgotten nothing since his salad days in price control during the war. He advocates introducing into the USA the whole dismal catalogue of measures—reducing the role of the money supply in economic policy, steeply progressive taxation, nationalization, price and wage controls and central economic planning —which have had such disastrous effects in Great Britain since 1945.[1] Without any analysis of the problems involved we are assured that there must be "a large and stable [sic!] flow of public expenditure"; and, what might come as a surprise to many of us in Britain, that "expenditures that reflect the public cognizance are categorically more efficient than those that serve the interests of the planning system". In tablets of stone Galbraith hews out as unequivocal propositions which are coming under increased questioning in the United Kingdom. With no signposts to explain the meaning of the words he instructs us that the level of public expenditure is given by the need for public services and it is the level so established that sets the level of taxation. "If demand is excessive, the generally appropriate procedure will be to increase taxes. The required level of public outlays has been decided on the basis of needs". And if taxes are already excessive and stultifying enterprise as in Britain? There is no discussion of this problem at all.

This is the same emotional and irrational approach to public expenditure that has done so much to impede objective discussion of the subject in the United Kingdom. Like the religion of ancient Rome, public expenditure has become holy ground;[2] he who treads upon it calls down the vengeance of the powerful beings for whom it has been set apart. Yet even in the considerable range of public expenditure for which there is no credible alternative—defence, maintenance of law and order, the enforcement of anti-monopoly legislation, the maintenance of environmental standards, and so forth—constant vigilance is essential to ensure that the proceeds of taxes are efficiently spent. But there are many other activities—health, housing, refuse disposal, libraries, parking and roads for example—where it is entirely legitimate to probe whether these should be provided by the general body of taxpayers or paid for, in whole or in part, by those who use the facilities.[3] Even if it is held that certain goods and services should be provided to the population at large, it is far from axiomatic that the most efficient way of doing so is directly through central or local governments.

There is a certain reluctance to challenge anyone who claims that a particular line of expenditure is in the national interest. In spite of its noble, unselfish ring it has too often become a refuge for charlatans and humbugs as well as an excuse for financial extravagance. It is not only Louis XIV and General Amin who have claimed—with differing degrees of linguistic elegance—that they are the State. Many groups and individuals have no great difficulty in defining the national interest in terms of their own personal scale of values and judgments.

There are those who would love to see an end of the top hat parades at Ascot but never seem to denounce the high cost of football players, the large tax-free rewards that flow from football pools or the many hundreds of millions of pounds spent annually in gambling in the United Kingdom.[4] Galbraith himself shows a great contempt for the tastes of many of his fellow Americans, particularly when they manifest themselves in the purchase of consumer products such as large and flashy cars with high tail fins. He writes about them in terms which would do credit to a Scottish Presbyterian Minister in hot pursuit of sin.

Now Ascot, football matches and large finned American cars have no attractions for many people; but those who do enjoy them should surely be allowed to do so. Such activities are as harmless as Mr Wedgwood Benn's amiable eccentricity of imbibing large quantities of tea from a drinking vessel of such noble proportions that it could well be used for other purposes. Under the shadow of a red banner which, according to mythology, has been held high at every major occasion from the sacking of Rome and the storming of the Bastille to the January sales in Oxford Street, Mr Benn conducts his tea ceremony with the finesse and delicacy normally associated with the Occident. Danger does not spring from such charming activities. It comes from the latter day Robespierres and *sans culottes* who convince themselves that their tastes are superior, that they know better than wage and salary earners what is good for them and are prepared to enforce their judgments in the name of the public interest. John Jewkes rightly pointed out many years ago that constant appeals to a public interest, which is either vaguely defined or not at all, usually flow from an outlook which is basically totalitarian in nature. Those who justify increasing public expenditure in the national interest have had their arguments accepted too readily. They should be subjected to critical scrutiny.

There are, of course, no absolutes about how much of a taxpayer's gross remuneration should be taken from him in exactions by central and local governments any more than there are absolutes about the percentage of net remuneration a wage or salary earner should provide his wife for domestic purposes. The benefits and expenses of the latter are, however, more visible and fairly easily calculable. The cost/benefit relations of government social expenditure, which subsidizes both individuals and services, are almost completely fogbound. Part of the fog is generated by the copious use of the word 'free' and the widespread belief, already mentioned, that politicians have some mystical means of making costs disappear.[5] But as Milton Friedman has pointed out: "there is no such thing as a free ride with governments in the driving seat".[6] Again we have been assured that increases in public expenditure can be rendered painless by using the resources created by accelerated growth—that holy grail which has always been just around the next corner but one for the last thirty years. When these two arguments fail to impress, vast phantom armies of the rich are conjured up from the deep to carry the heavy load. Unfortunately there are not enough rich people to go around.

Now it could well be that the electorate would prefer a higher social wage at the expense of having less money in their pockets to spend as they wish. What has been clear for a long time is that it is impossible to have both on anything like the scale that has been represented as attainable by some of our so-called public leaders. Living beyond one's intellectual income is a common enough human frailty; some politicians do it on a massive scale and make grandiose promises which exceed by a substantial margin their capacity to deliver. "We have turned our backs on the economics of scarcity" said Herbert Morrison in 1946 with his usual tremulous vibrations. Judging by the conditions prevailing some three decades later scarcity does not seem to have paid too much attention to his contemptuous gesture. It is this jingoistic approach that contributes so much to obscuring the fact that the electorate is faced with questions of choice: of how best to use the scarce resources to meet the wide range of demands imposed upon them; of how much personal income should accrue to the government and how much should be retained for personal disposal. These basic problems will remain part of the lot of man until someone lifts, or erases, the curse of Adam.

Governments which are unable or unwilling to raise the necessary revenue or tap genuine savings to finance expenditure usually finish by resorting to the printing press.[7] It is the most arbitrary form of all taxation. It is also the last refuge of political cowardice. True, an increase in the money supply on the scale that took place in Britain in the 1970s can, for a brief period of time, create the illusion that Herbert Morrison tried to encourage. The ultimate cost of such folly in terms of inflation and unemployment is being borne by the people of Britain today and the end is not yet in sight.[8] The issues have seldom been put honestly to the electorate; yet most housewives, if not some politicians, know full well that the contents of a pint measure will not fill a quart bottle.

It is far from being axiomatic, as Galbraith assumes, that the State as a provider of various services is a highly efficient operator. Hardly a week passes without publicity for some case or other involving abuse of the social security system,[9] or examples of government ineptitude which, if perpertrated by a private company, would ensure that it would soon be out of business and deservedly so.

Bureaucracy proliferates. Water rates which used to be charged with general rates are now billed separately; more letters have to be mailed, more cheques signed, more records have to be kept and more accountants and clerks employed than under the previous simplified collection system. A grant is made from public funds for a post-graduate to learn to play chess with a computer and to an 'artist' to travel around sweeping piles of dirt into artistic formations. Ratepayers subsidize courses in wine tasting and the cost per person using some of the vast sports complexes that have been constructed around the country without much sign of co-ordination must be very high indeed. The people engaged in information services in central and local governments are out of all proportion to the nature or quality of the information available for distribution; while the use of the taxpayers' money to prop up the motor cycle industry and a Scottish newspaper,[10] to take only two examples, has given cause for widespread concern.

The catalogue could be continued almost indefinitely—indeed one responsible Sunday newspaper has decided to record examples continuously and in depth during 1977. As Lord Rothschild, formerly in charge of research in the Royal Dutch/Shell Group and first head of the Government's Central Policy Review Staff (the "Think Tank") put it: "If people would stop talking about cutting public expenditure and substitute elimination of waste, life would be a good deal easier".

Government expenditure in the United Kingdom, depending on how the calculations are made, now accounts for between 50 and 60 per cent of the gross national product compared to under 40 per cent ten years ago.[11] The growth has been rapid and in absolute terms has now reached £60,000m per annum. When, at the opening of the Strathclyde Business School at the end of 1976, I stated that it would be very surprising if a performance and efficiency audit over the whole range of government expenditure would not disclose, over a period, potential savings of 5 to 10 per cent, several people suggested that the estimate of possible savings was too low. However, even 5 to 10 per cent—£3,000/£6,000m—would make a sizeable contribution. But the inbuilt resistance to such reductions should not be underestimated.

In contrast to Galbraith, Adam Smith's lack of faith in the ability of governments to spend wisely is illustrated in his oft-quoted phrase, "Kings and Ministers . . . are themselves always and without any exception the greatest spendthrifts in the society. Let them well look after their own expenses and they may safely trust private people with theirs".[12] The Scottish sage firmly believed that in the satisfaction of human wants money was most advantageously spent by those who had actually earned it. The further spending was removed from the point of earning, the less the responsibility with which it was handled. There are plenty of examples to sustain the generality of Smith's thesis and very little from recent British experience to support Galbraith's somewhat blind faith in the intrinsic superiority of public over private expenditure.

Notes

1. George and Priscilla Polanyi, *Failing the Nation: The Record of the Nationalised Industries*, Fraser Ansbacher, 1974, *Planning in Britain: the Experience of the 1960's*, Institute of Economic Affairs, 1967; Samuel Brittan and Peter Lilley, *The Delusion of Incomes Policy*, Maurice Temple Smith; David Morgan, *Over-Taxation by Inflation*, Institute of Economic Affairs, 1977; A.A. Walters, *Money in Boom and Slump*, Institute of Economic Affairs, 1965.
2. *The dilemmas of Government Expenditure*, Essays by economists and parliamentarians, Institute of Economic Affairs, 1976.
3. A.K. Maynard and D.N. King, *Rates or Prices?*, Institute of Economic Affairs, 1972; R. Harris and A. Seldon, *Pricing or Taxing?*, Institute of Economic Affairs, 1976; A. Seldon, *Charge*, Maurice Temple Smith, 1977.
4. *Report of the Gaming Board for Great Britain 1975*, House of Commons Paper 237, HMSO, 1976.
5. G.H. Peters, *Cost-Benefit Analysis and Public Expenditure*, Institute of Economic Affairs, 1966 (3rd Edition, 1972).
6. *An Economist's Protest*, Thomas Horton, 1972.
7. Chancellors include Dalton, Butler, Amory, Maudling and Barber.
8. R. Harris and B. Sewill, *British Economic Policy 1970-74; Two Views*, Institute of Economic Affairs, 1975.
9. 'How Benefit Fiddles are Spreading', *The Sunday Telegraph*, 18 July, 1976.
10. *National Enterprise Board*, 1976.
11. *National Income and Expenditure 1965-75*, HMSO, 1976.
12. *The Wealth of Nations* (Edited by Edwin Cannan), Vol. I, pp. 367, Methuen, 1961.

VIII. Overall Planning on the Planning System

Based on his assessment of how the planning system operates in large corporations, Galbraith deems it quite unnecessary to establish a case for ousting the market economy by centralized economic planning. To him it is all self-evident. And there is all the usual jargon. The State "will impose overall planning on the planning system . . . Government machinery must be established to anticipate disparity and to ensure that growth in different parts of the economy is compatible". In a flight of fancy reminiscent of the communique issued after Kosygin's visit to London some ten years ago[1] we are informed that there must be "co-ordination of planning policies as between national planning systems. This must include common policies in the distribution of capital as between industries; common steps to control the wages price spiral"; and "National planning systems operating internationally also require a measure of international planning".

Anyone who has taken part in the planning process in a large corporation or who has endeavoured to obtain international accord over a limited range of topics realizes that these lofty views of Galbraith are unreal and totally impractical. A few of the difficulties which confront corporate planners have already been mentioned; these are multiplied many-fold when the process is elevated to the national—let alone the international—level. If, as Galbraith says, one of the functions of national planners is to pass judgment on the compatibility of the plans of various industries, it is necessary that the whole process starts off with common assumptions about some of the basic factors likely to unfold in the economy as a whole—for example, growth in output, inflation rates, balance of payments' trends and unemployment. But what is the process of selecting these figures and who does it? The table below gives five forecasts for Great Britain for the years 1976-77.

TABLE 5

	Output growth %		Inflation %		Balance of payments £m		Unemployment (millions) end end	
	1976	1977	1976	1977	1976	1977	1976	1977
London Business School	2.2	4.0	15.6	9.7	−1980	−1800	−	−
Phillips & Drew	0.9	1.8	16.6	14.8	−1875	−1250	1.3	1.5
Henley Centre	2.9	3.0	14.1	10.5	−2000	−2200	1.5	1.5
NIESR	1.0	1.7	15.5	13.2	−1700	1100	1.3	1.3
DataSTREAM International	2.1	0.8	15.9	17.3	−1750	−768	1.3	1.7

Given the size of the aggregates in such a wide range it is obvious that we are going to be living in a very different Britain if the growth in output in 1977 is only 0.8 per cent—the lowest forecast—rather than 4 per cent —the highest. It would be quite possible to construct another twenty or so estimates, some with even wider variations than those quoted above, but all of equal plausibility, while the further the time horizon is pushed forward, the more divergent is likely to be the range of the forecasts. Since there is no objective reason for favouring one of these projections over the others, it is difficult to see the justification for erecting an enormous statistical edifice showing how every aspect of the economy is estimated to perform. Nor is it only the foundations which are arbitrary and incapable of carrying any load: every structural member is shaky and suspect.[2]

The strength of the foundations become even more doubtful when, almost inevitably, the selection of the basic figures is in the hands of governments. Here we are up against one of the many fundamental dilemmas of all economic planning. The nature of politics is such that, quite irrespective of the surrounding facts, no government can plan over its theoretical period of office to have a lower growth rate than the historical trend line. This would be to confess in advance the stark failures that we now tend only to see with the passage of time. Nor, of course, can governments really plan for a continuation of the historical rate of growth; there would be too strong a presumption that this would be achieved without their 'intermeddling' at all in the market place. So governments have to plan for a rate of growth above the trend line. But what higher rate, how determined and, even more important, how is it to be achieved? It is this sort of dilemma—to which there is no ready answer—that produces the superficially gallant, but quite meaningless, statements from the NEDC about low rates of growth being "totally unacceptable".[3]

West Germany[4] and Singapore, to take two examples, believe in the efficacy of a social market economy. Although widely divergent in resources and social attitudes, the populations of both countries have enjoyed greater improvements in their standards of living than those achieved by most other states. Within a defined legal framework, including laws to enforce social objectives that can only be achieved provided everyone complies, both governments accept the basic truth of Adam Smith's dictum that "the uniform, constant and uninterrupted effort of every man to better his condition [is] the principle from which public and national, as well as private, opulence is originally derived ... "[5] It has certainly proved successful in both these countries.

Perhaps some of Professor Galbraith's supporters would have the planning bug flushed out of their systems had they stood on the roof of one of Singapore's skyscrapers just after dawn and viewed the hundred of thousands of people going industriously about their business; the shipyards and manufacturing plants in operation; one of the largest oil refinery complexes in the world, turning out products to balance the Far East supply pattern; the large container terminals and the armada of sampans carrying goods to and from the ships lying offshore. It is a small island—most of it is visible. Apart from items like atomic power stations, virtually every commodity grown or manufactured in the world passes through Singapore. All that takes place in this hive of economic activity, both trading and manufacturing, is literally the result of millions of individual decisions taken over time both in Singapore and other parts of the world—decisions which are integrated and brought to final fruition by the operation of the market economy. It could only be arrogance or, to use Mr James Callaghan's phrase, total and abysmal ignorance, that would prompt any economist or politician to claim that they could plan this wide range of activities in any meaningful sense of the term.

If any remaining planning illusions lingered on, a visit to the Singapore Prime Minister or his deputy should assist in finally dispersing them. Dr Goh Keng Swee expresses his views with lucidity: "When we first won the elections we had no plans at all. We produced a formal document called the First Four-Year Plan in 1960 only because the World Bank wanted a plan. We cooked it up during a long week-end". After an amusing account of the history of the planning unit, Dr Goh continues: "Then in 1965 the planning Unit produced a wonderful Five-

Year Plan which was very well printed. It went to the Cabinet soon after the split with Malaysia . . . and all the plans made in the beautiful volume were totally irrelevant . . . This was the last of our planning efforts" Dr Goh rightly emphasizes that it is economic policy, not planning, that is the key issue; he enunciates three principles as a basis for success:

First, always balance your budget. We never print paper money as a means of paying for government expenditure . . .

Secondly, have an open competitive system. Allow talent and enterprise to rise and earn their due rewards . . . the businessman knows what is best for himself and it is not for government to tell him what to do.

Thirdly, go for growth and all things necessary to support that growth. Provide the infrastructure, make sure skilled labour is available; this means reshaping the education system.[6]

No doubt some of the more intricate minds that have contributed so generously to retarding economic growth in Britain will regard Dr Goh's prescription for success as over-simplified. But if, as enjoined by the Holy Writ, the tree is to be judged by its fruit, the success in West Germany as well as Singapore seems unchallengeable. It has never really been given a chance to flourish in post-war Britain; the so-called "bonfires of controls" were always too modest in concept.

The acceptance of the principles of a market economy still leaves a considerable role for governments not only in their traditional functions but as creators of the general framework within which industry must operate. These include matters such as pollution standards, and the provision of safety nets for those who by virtue of age or health or lack of employment are unable to earn a livelihood. Beyond that governments should create an environment that will lend positive encouragement to economic growth. That rate of growth should, however, be allowed to look after itself; too many politicians and civil servants have been playing God in the market place for too long; since they lack the divine knowledge to discharge the role, they usually finish up by looking silly and pretentious whether it be in relation to the 1965 Economic Plan or the price of bread in 1977.

Of course it would be wrong to suggest that the market mechanism is flawless. It is not, but it has fewer flaws than any of the alternatives available. Those who dislike the profit motive are free under a market system to establish co-operatives; the consumer is equally free to shop there or at the vast range of stores established and managed by private enterprise. The market mechanism co-ordinates much more speedily than any alternative the vast range of adjustments, which take place every day, in supply, demand and prices. It enables workers to follow the occupations of their choice, not as dictated by some bureaucrat so remote from the coal face that he has to view all operatives as statistics.

The market economy and the freedoms it embraces are under attack from several quarters including left-wing politicians and their economic planning allies who lay claim to knowledge and clairvoyance they simply do not possess.[7] Galbraith is one of the more articulate and vocal of the attackers, but when his rhetoric is stripped away the emperor seems to have little else in the way of clothes. We are left with a series of intemperate generalizations. Not only are they unsupported by any facts, they are contradicted by such evidence as is available. Had Professor Galbraith strayed from the Victorian precincts of Raffles Hotel during his televised visit to Singapore his symbiotic link with central economic planning might well have been terminated and in its place a new symbiosis established with the market economy—and the threat of blight would be partially lifted from the land.

Notes   *Read Galbraith!*

1. The two Prime Ministers agreed that "it was desirable to develop longer term arrangements related to the forward planning of their productive economies to enable, on both sides, the development of productive capacity for expanding trade in both directions". Come ten ten years or so later the first progress report on this absurd proposition is still awaited.
2. George Polanyi, *Short-Term Forecasting: A Case Study,* Institute of Economic Affairs, 1973.
3. (The reader interested in the pretensions of the would-be planners should read Professor John Jewkes, *The New Ordeal by Planning,* Macmillan, 1968.)
4. Ludwig Erhard, *Prosperity Through Competition,* Thames and Hudson, 1958.
5. *op.cit.,* Vol. I, pp. 364.
6. *This Singapore.*
7. Stuart Holland's *The Socialist Challenge,* Quartet Books, 1975; *Strategy for Socialism: The Challenge of Labour's Programme,* Bertrand Russell Peace Foundation for Spokesman Books, 1975.